**WILDE'S**
*LEISURE GUIDES*

# CYCLE ROUTE GUIDE
## TO 19 LEISURE TRAILS

# LANCASHIRE
# & THE LAKE DISTRICT

*Written by*
**Gillian Rowan-Wilde**

Published by
GILDERSLEVE
PUBLISHING LIMITED

# GENERAL INFORMATION

Wilde's Leisure Guides are a trade mark of Gildersleve Publishing Ltd.

© Copyright Gillian Rowan-Wilde

Published by
Gildersleve Publishing Ltd
Capricorn House, Blackburn Road
Rising Bridge, Lancashire BB5 2AA

ACKNOWLEDGMENTS
*To Peter Rodgers of the Lake District Ranger Service for his help in checking the routes. Paul Gildersleve for his "tree planting."*
*John Beatty for donating our cover picture and last but not least the originators of all the trails without which it would have been impossible to start this journey.*
*Maps based upon Ordnance Survey mapping with the permission of the Controller of Her Majesty's Stationery Office,*
*© Crown copyright.*

## THE OFFROAD CYCLING CODE

**STAY ON THE TRAIL**
Only ride bridleways & byways
Avoid footpaths
Plan your route in advance
**GIVE WAY TO HORSES & WALKERS**
Make sure you are heard when riding up behind anyone
Ride carefully, keep to the left of anyone approaching you.
**NEVER RIDE IN LARGE GROUPS**
5 or 6 is maximum
**BE KIND TO BIRDS, ANIMALS & PLANTS**
Keep your dog under control
**PREVENT EROSION**
Avoid skidding and locking your wheels when braking.
**CLOSE GATES BEHIND YOU**
Don't climb walls or force hedges
**EQUIPMENT FOR SAFETY**
Wear a helmet
Take a first aid kit
Carry enough food and drink
Pack waterproofs & warm clothes
Take essential spares & tools
**TAKE PRIDE IN YOUR BIKE**
Maintain your bike before you leave, and on your return.
**BE TIDY**
Take all your litter home
Never create a fire hazard
**ENJOY YOUR CYCLING**
Try not to get annoyed with anyone, it never solves a problem Don't make unnecessary noise

## RIGHTS OF WAY

Off-road cyclists have right of way on most public bridleways and other tracks unless forbidden by a bye-law. You must give way to walkers and horseriders.

By-ways, which are usually unsurfaced tracks are open to cyclists, as well as walkers and horseriders, you may also find vehicles have right to access.

There is NO right of way on Public Footpaths, if cyclists finds themselves on a public footpath they must get off their bike and walk.

A cyclist is NOT permitted to ride his bike on the pavements.

On moorland, upland or farmland a cyclist normally has NO right of access without the express permission of the landowner.

Tow-paths by the canals normally require a permit from the appropriate British Waterways.

There are quite a few designated cycle routes and paths to be found in urban areas, on Waterways tow-paths, Forestry Commission land or on disused railway lines.

Cyclists must adhere to the Highway Code.

## GENERAL SAFETY HINTS

1. Make sure your bike is safe to ride before leaving home. It is adviseable to take with you a puncture repair kit, a spare inner tube, and the necessary spanners and levers to help with your repair. Don't forget your pump!
2. You must by law display working lights after dark.
3. Always carry some form of identification.
4. Always tell someone where you are going.
5. Learn the basic principles of first aid and take a small first aid kit.
6. Wear reflective material on your clothes, better to be seen.
7. Ride under control when going down hill, accidents can happen.
8. It is adviseable to always wear a helmet.
9. Carry a water bottle, always keep it filled especially on a hot day. Take spare food, drink and clothing with you.
10. Be very careful when riding on marsh land or scree especially when it is wet.
11. Always take a detailed map with you for adventurous or wilderness trips. Have a compass with you. Take a whistle with you to use when calling for help should you have an accident.
12. Always be aware of others using the same path as yourself. They also want to enjoy their day out!
13. General maintenance of your bike on your return home. Making sure it is cleaned and oiled ready for your next trip.

# CONTENTS

# TRAIL LOCATION MAP

Trail *(page No)* — Lancashire

Area of Lake District National Park — Cumbria

# KEY

 Information Centre

 Parking

 Public Convenience

 Telephone

 Picnic Area

 Camp Site

 Caravan Site

 Public House/Hotel

 Boating

 Church

 Built up Area

Marsh

Cycle Trail

Main Road

Minor Road

Footpath

Railway Track

National Park Boundary

River/Stream

Lake/Reservoir

 Mixed Wood

 Coniferous Wood

 Points of Interest

 Mountain Profile View Point

3

## ABOUT THE AUTHOR

*Gillian Rowan-Wilde took up leisure cycling in the summer of 1993, her first trail being the Tarka Trail which she undertook during a holiday in Devon. Since then she has ridden most of the trails in the North West.*

*As well as cycling she is an accomplished fell and mountain walker and a member of the long Distance Walkers Association. Among her accomplishments as a walker, are the completion of one of the '100' mile walks, Mountain Marathons and numerous challenge walks over 30 miles.*

*She has completed courses at Glencoe in Scotland on rock and ice climbing also survival techniques whilst on the mountains with instructors from the Crowden Outdoor Pursuits Centre.*

*In this series of guides she hopes to bring to the leisure cyclist a catalogue of historical and interesting features on rides, together with some of the wildlife you may encounter.*

**WILDE'S**
LEISURE GUIDES

## MAPS BY

*Andy Thelwell has grown up with Apple Macs and computer graphics. At present he is employed as a technical manager with a leading north west art studio*

*In his spare time he is either in the gym, or out off-road on his mountain bike.*

## ILLUSTRATION BY

*Graham Nicholson studied illustration at Lincoln, since then he has been commissioned by many leading national, and international companies, supplying work for packaging, advertising campaign's and corporate brochures.*

*In his leisure time he is a keen walker, an interest he shares with his family.*

# INTRODUCTION

If you think that cycling is all traffic fumes and road noises and that the Lake District is now overrun with tourists, then this book will make you think again. Our off-road cycling guide will surprise and delight even regular visitors at a cyclist's pace and in an environment well away from all but the quietest of roads.

In this guide we have compiled a varied selection of some of the most interesting trails in Lancashire and the Lake District. Unlike our first guide, where most trails used disused railways, this time we guide you upward through forest and moorland. This means that many of the routes are more challenging rides through undulating country, but we hope that you'll find that the spectacular views more than compensate for the climbs. For those who prefer a more leisurely ride, we've also included some trails that follow canals, estuaries and old railway lines.

Each route has it's own custom-drawn map showing everything you need to know from distances and directions to parking, picnic and rest stops. In addition to our popular illustrations of the plant and animal life you may see along each route, we've also included skyline identification charts to help you get the most from the views from the high points of the hillier rides.

So come deer watching with us in the Gisburn Forest and follow the heron along the Leeds/Liverpool canal. What ever your ability or age, we're sure our guide will help you get the most from a day spent off-road in the Lakes - and if you haven't got a bike we've marked the best hire centres in the area so you can try before you buy.

If you get half as much pleasure from using this guide as we did in researching it, then you'll surely become as hooked on the joys of off-road cycling as we are.

Happy trails.

*Peter*

Peter Gildersleve

# PACKING YOUR ESSENTIALS

There are various packs, bags and panniers available today in fact for some it can be difficult to know what to use and where to carry them.

Illustrated are a number of carrying positions for different capacities of bags. In addition to these there are a variety of touring front and rear panniers available. Coming from a walking background I prefer to use a small daysac in which I carry my food and waterproofs with a bar bag on the bike which usually has my tool kit, chocolate, maps and camera. Other people I know prefer to keep their body free and carry everything on their bikes - so you should do which ever feels comfortable.

Bar Bag • Bum Bag • Rucksack

Bar Bag • Rack Pack

Stem Bag • Wedge Bag • Seat Bag

# WHAT TO WEAR - SUMMER OR WINTER

We all know just how unpredictable our weather can be, you may begin your day warm, and within hours be very cold. The best way to prepare for any eventuality is to layer your clothing so that as the day progresses you can maintain a balance between being either too hot or too cold.

Your first layer, should be made from a fabric that takes the moisture away from your body so that you don't get that cold clammy feeling, as you do when wearing a cotton t-shirt. The next layer must be a warm one preferably a fleece with a longer 'tail' to keep your back warm as you bend over the handlebars. Your trousers should not be too baggy otherwise the leg fabric could get caught up in your cycle chain. Padded cycling shorts and underwear are available, ideal for a day in the saddle.

A windproof jacket is essential as it keeps the wind chill away, since they are made of light weight fabric they can easily be tucked away in a pocket or small bag. Your waterproof layer should comprise of both jacket and trousers preferably made from a breathable fabric.

Mittens or gloves which have a padded palm help absorb the shocks of the bumps and of course a well fitting helmet is essential.

*Pausing to view in Gisburn Forest.*

# TRAIL GRADING

*All trails have the O.S. map nos. given for guidance, so that the areas can be easily identified*

## EASY

*Old railway tracks   Towpaths on canals/rivers*
*No hills*

## EASY, ADVENTUROUS

*As above but with a hill - easily negotiable*

## MODERATE

*Forest paths   Lakeside   Moorland*
A hill, stream or rough ground - easily negotiable

## MODERATE, ADVENTUROUS

*As above but possibly more than one hill - easily negotiable*

## HARD

*Fells or Forests with hills*
Several hills with a degree of difficulty and ground may be undulating

## HARD, ADVENTUROUS

*As above but with longer hills and steeper gradients*

## SEVERE

*High, steep hills and fells*
Very hilly and ground exceptionally difficult

# DUNSOP BRIDGE
## FOREST OF BOWLAND

DUNSOP BRIDGE IS SITUATED TO THE EAST OF THE TROUGH OF BOWLAND WITH THE RIVER HODDER TO THE SOUTH. TO THE NORTH IS THE OFFICIAL ORDNANCE SURVEY CENTRE OF BRITAIN SITED ON BROWN SYKE MOSS.

**The Bowland Fells are the largest area of continuous heatherland in Lancashire and Dunsop Bridge lies at the foot of the 'Feather Bed' the old name for the Trough of Bowland. The original village of Dunsop was sited at Beatrix until the 18th century.**

| | |
|---|---|
| **START & FINISH:** [S] | Dunsop Bridge |
| **MAP:** | O.S. Landranger Series No. 103 (Blackburn and Burnley) |
| **LENGTH(approx):** | 13km (8 ½m) Circular |
| **SURFACE:** | Tarmac, moorland grass |
| **RIDE RATING :** | Moderate |

*NOTE: Do not stray from the track as there are lead mine shafts and openings in the area.*

KILOMETRES

STATUTE MILES

The trail from Dunsop Bridge is a combination of beautiful valley scenery beside the River Dunsop and the Brennand River and the wild moorland of Middle Knoll where there are the remains of old lead mines.

At Dunsop Bridge there is a telephone box (A), encircled by four wooden posts showing the main points of the compass. This is the place marked by British Telecom as their 'Centre of Britain'.

The Forest of Bowland with its regimented rows of conifers is not the reason for the area being known as a Forest. The word 'Forest' is derived from the Latin word 'Foris' meaning 'out of doors' a word used for Royal Hunting Grounds rather than an area of trees. In the 10th century the county of Lancashire was held by the Norwegians, hence the Norse names in the area. One instance is the name Beatrix which comes from 'Bothvar's Ergh' meaning a hill farm belonging to Bothvar. Today the main landowners of Bowland are the Duke of Westminster, the Crown and the regional water authority.

The word 'Brennand' used frequently in the area west of Middle Knoll means 'the burning one'. It is thought that this meaning came about by the settlers seeing the bright rays of the sun setting over Morecambe Bay shining between the hills and ravines and lighting up the fell on Middle Knoll (B) *as though it was on fire.*

At Brennand Farm (C) the path up the side of Middle Knoll is steep but once on level ground there are stunning views on a clear day. The path is marked by yellow signposts and very easy to follow down to Whitendale. Before descending to Whitendale there is a small reservoir and pit head (D) The water was used to supply power to the waterwheels for the mines up on the hill which were last worked in 1874.

Once in Whitendale (E), meaning 'The dale of the White Line (heather)', turn right keeping Whitendale river on your left and follow the track around the east side of Middle Knoll to the confluence of the rivers Whitendale and Brennand (F) and back down the valley to Dunsop Bridge.

*Red Grouse and Common Gorse.*

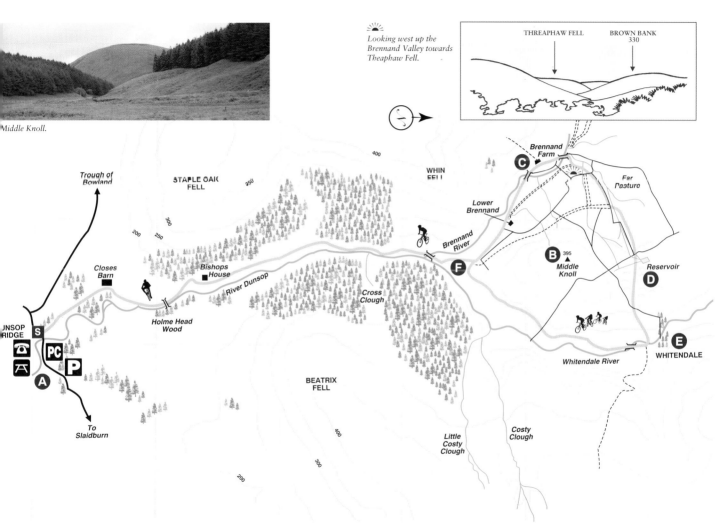

Middle Knoll.

Looking west up the Brennand Valley towards Theaphaw Fell.

THREAPHAW FELL     BROWN BANK 330

Trough of Bowland

STAPLE OAK FELL

400

250

WHIN FELL

Brennand Farm

C

Lower Brennand

Far Pasture

300

200   250

Closes Barn

Bishops House

River Dunsop

Brennand River

F

B   395
Middle Knoll

Reservoir

D

Holme Head Wood

Cross Clough

E

WHITENDALE

UNSOP RIDGE

S

PC

P

A

Whitendale River

BEATRIX FELL

To Slaidburn

Little Costy Clough

Costy Clough

400

300

200

9

# GISBURN FOREST

GISBURN FOREST IS SITUATED ON THE NORTH EAST BOUNDARY OF LANCASHIRE WITH N. YORKSHIRE. TO THE WEST IS STOCKS RESERVOIR AND THE RIVER HODDER AND TO THE SOUTH THE B6478 BETWEEN SLAIDBURN AND LONG PRESTON.

**Gisburn Forest has seen a lot of felling and planting of new trees over the last few years. The views as you ride through the forest of the rolling hills and Stocks Reservoir are magnificent.**

| START & FINISH: **S** | Cocklet Hill Car Park |
|---|---|
| MAP: | O.S. Landranger Series No. 103 (Blackburn and Burnley) |
| LENGTH (approx): | 2 main routes approx. 11km (7m) each. Both circular routes |
| SURFACE: | Gravel, tarmac |
| RIDE RATING : | Easy, adventurous |

NOTE: *Please keep on the hard surfaced tracks within the Forest.*

KILOMETRES | | 1 | 2 |
STATUTE MILES | | 1 |

There are three main entrances into the forest, either from the village of Tosside (**A**) or from either of the two car parks (**B&C**) on the Trough of Bowland road.

The Village of Tosside stands astride the Lancashire and North Yorkshire boundary, and well worth a visit. A great many of the buildings were originally built from the Bowland stone, but now only one or two 17th century pieces are left. On entering the Forest down the track beside the Dog & Partridge, on your left before the woodmill there is a wooden gate leading to an enchanting ride through the forest past a stream tumbling into a small pond. A very tranquil and beautiful place to stop and enjoy the peaceful surroundings.

From the top of the Car park at Cocklet Hill (**B**) you will see a stoney path seemingly disappearing into the trees. It is a bit bumpy but you eventually arrive at a 'T' junction where you turn left down to the next junction and turn right to the impressive farmstead of Stephen Park (**D**). The house stands in a very tranquil setting amongst the pines, built in 1662 on the site of a hunting lodge. Opposite the house stands the old coach house with beautiful archways. Straight up the track will eventually bring you to a junction. Turn right for the village of Tosside or left to pass the farmstead of Hesbert Hall (**E**) with a '1673' datestone built into the stone of the Hall. All other buildings around are now only ruins. Cross the ford at Dob Dale Beck (**F**) and up the hill to view the whole area of forest. Turn right and follow the track to School Lane. Turn left but be careful; this road is very steep down to the car park on the right as the road corners left beside Stocks Reservoir.

Stocks in Dalehead was a tiny Hamlet until 1922 when the River Hodder was dammed and the area became Stocks Reservoir. Further along the road you will be able to see the full expanse of the reservoir from the Causeway with the island in the middle, often covered with a very noisy colony of breeding Black-Headed Gulls. The tiny church of Dalehead (**G**) is on a remote site beside the road and is a memorial to the old community now submerged. The church was built in 1938 from the stones of the old village church and the graves were moved to the present churchyard.

**LANCASHIRE**

Slaidburn · Gisburn
Newton · B6478
Clitheroe · Colne
32 · A59
31 · Burnley
M65
30 · Blackburn
M61

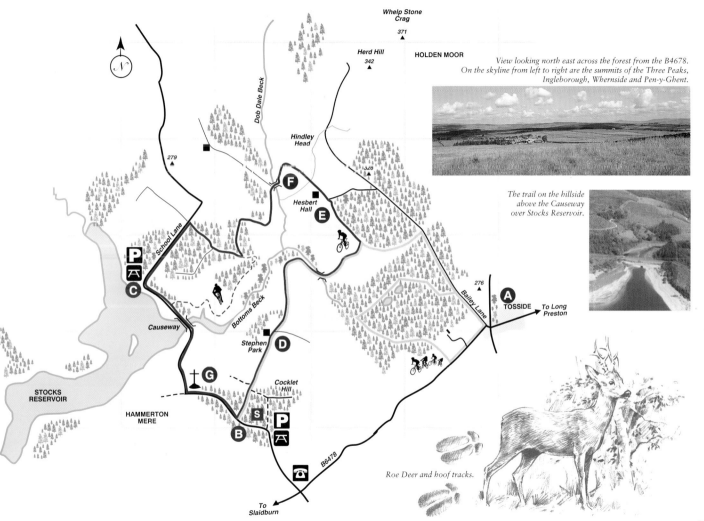

Whelp Stone Crag
371

Herd Hill
342

HOLDEN MOOR

Dob Dale Beck

Hindley Head

326

Hesbert Hall

**F**

**E**

279

School Lane

**P**

**C**

Causeway

Bottoms Beck

Stephen Park

**D**

STOCKS RESERVOIR

**G**

Cocklet Hill

HAMMERTON MERE

**S**

**P**

**B**

B6478

To Slaidburn

276

Bailey Lane

**A**
TOSSIDE

To Long Preston

*View looking north east across the forest from the B4678.*
*On the skyline from left to right are the summits of the Three Peaks,*
*Ingleborough, Whernside and Pen-y-Ghent.*

*The trail on the hillside above the Causeway over Stocks Reservoir.*

*Roe Deer and hoof tracks.*

11

# GLASSON CIRCULAR

THE GLASSON CIRCULAR IS SITUATED BETWEEN THE RIVER LUNE TO THE WEST, LANCASTER
TO THE NORTH, THE M6 TO THE EAST AND THE RIVER CONDOR TO THE SOUTH

The Glasson Circular trail follows the coastal path to Lancaster using the
route of the old Lancaster-Glasson railway line which closed in 1964.
In Lancaster you join the Lancaster Canal towpath by way of the
Lune Aquaduct which carries the Canal over the River Lune.
At Galgate the path follows a branch of the canal into Glasson.

| START & FINISH: | S | Glasson on the B5290 beside the canal basin. |
|---|---|---|
| MAP: | | O.S. Landranger Series No.102 (Preston, and Blackpool) |
| | | O.S. Landranger Series No.97 (Kendal and Morecambe) |
| LENGTH (approx): | | 26km ( 17m) Circular |
| SURFACE: | | Grass, gravel, tarmac |
| RIDE RATING: | | Easy |

NOTE: (alternate route) Before Marsh Point on New Quay Lane turn right to Aldcliffe.
In approx 1mile the road meets the Lancaster Canal. Turn right on the towpath to return
to Glasson.

KILOMETRES  1  2  3  4
STATUTE MILES  1  2

The trail begins in the town of Glasson, which grew rapidly when shipping was diverted from Lancaster as the River Lune began to silt up. A dock was built to help with this extra trade but merchants found it too difficult getting their goods to Lancaster. Glasson Dock's fortunes began to diminish, even though a canal was cut through to Galgate and later a railway built to help increase trade. With this decline the passenger service was withdrawn in 1930 and the freight line closed in 1947.

At Condor Green (**A**) the Crossing Keeper's Cottage and the bridge over the River Condor are among a few of the relics still to be seen of the old railway.

The mudflats and sandybanks of the river are a haven for wildlife. Sheep graze on the saltmarshes and wading birds come in to feed on the debris left by the tidal flow of the river.

As the trail meets the little used road at Marsh Point on the outskirts of Lancaster, the route takes you down St. George's Quay (**B**) past the old Customs House which is now a Maritime Museum. Turn right between the converted warehouses (Duke Street) (**C**), through a small car park at the rear of the buildings and keep straight ahead up the path to the 'T' junction. Turn left and follow this path to the Greyhound bridge and the River Lune. The cycleway signs take you under the road and through Green Ayre Riverside Park keeping the river on your left.

Once through the park follow the path (see 'Bull Beck to Lancaster' trail) until you reach the Lune Aquaduct. Negotiate the steps up onto the Aquaduct

(**D**), turn right and follow the canal towpath to Galgate. This canal section has some of the most varied and beautiful scenery of the whole route as it winds its way through the town, beside woods and into open countryside.

When you reach Galgate look for the branch of the canal coming in on your right which is signposted 'Glasson Spur' (**E**). This part of the canal to Glasson is quite uncultivated and enchanting. On this stretch you pass six locks and negotiate seven bridges in a relatively short distance. Finally pass the Marina on the canal basin at Glasson.

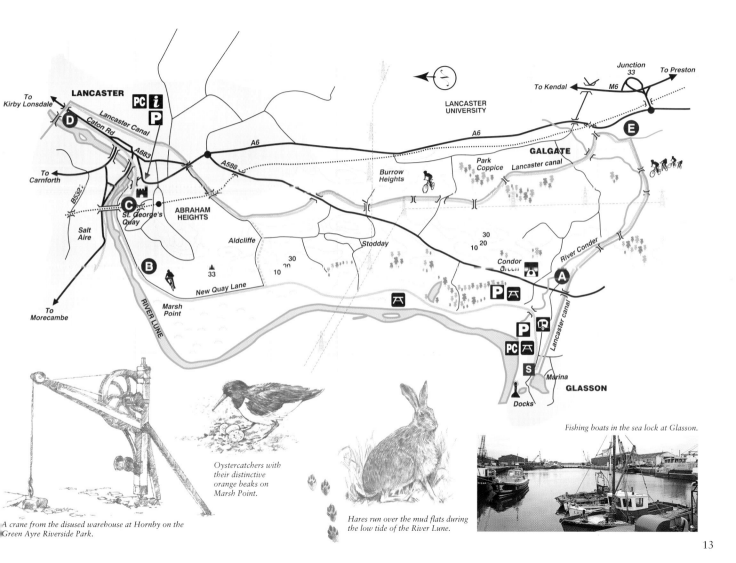

**To Kirby Lonsdale**

**LANCASTER**

PC · i
P

Lancaster Canal

Caton Rd

A683

**To Carnforth**

B5321

A588

A6

**LANCASTER UNIVERSITY**

**Junction 33**
**To Preston**

**To Kendal**

M6

Park Coppice

**GALGATE**

Lancaster canal

E

A6

Burrow Heights

C
St. George's Quay

Salt Aire

ABRAHAM HEIGHTS

Aldcliffe

Stodday

30
10 20

Condor Green

River Conder

Lancaster canal

A

B

33

New Quay Lane

30
10 20

**To Morecambe**

Marsh Point

RIVER LUNE

P ⊼

P
⊟
PC ⊼

S

Marina

Docks

**GLASSON**

*A crane from the disused warehouse at Hornby on the Green Ayre Riverside Park.*

*Oystercatchers with their distinctive orange beaks on Marsh Point.*

*Hares run over the mud flats during the low tide of the River Lune.*

*Fishing boats in the sea lock at Glasson.*

13

# BULL BECK-LANCASTER

This trail is situated between Bull Beck, near Caton Green and Lancaster, following the River Lune downstream. The A683 from Hornby to Lancaster has access to the M6 at Junction 34.

**The Bull Beck to Lancaster trail runs parallel with the River Lune along the route of the old Lancaster-Wennington railway line. In 1847 the North Western Railway Co. completed this Lancaster Branch line and when it was inaugurated in 1850 it reached as far as the fishing village of Poulton-le-Sands. When Poulton became popular as a bathing resort in 1900, the village changed its name to 'Morecambe' from the Bay.**

| | | |
|---|---|---|
| **START:** | S | Bull Beck Picnic Area on the A683 near Caton Green |
| **FINISH:** | | Green Ayre Riverside Park, Lancaster |
| **MAP:** | | O.S. Landranger Series No. 97 (Kendal and Morecambe) |
| **LENGTH** (approx): | | 9km (6m) Linear |
| **SURFACE:** | | Hard core, tarmac |
| **RIDE RATING:** | | Easy |

KILOMETRES | 1 2 3
STATUTE MILES | 1 2

The trail starts directly across the road from Bull Beck Car Park. The path takes you along the sand shingle banks of the River Lune. On a clear day looking in an easterly direction you can see the magnificent facade of Hornby Castle.

At Halton Green the views of the river and in the distance Ingleborough hill, are superb. The nature trail (footpath only) at the Crook O'Lune (A) takes you down to the water's edge where you can watch, amongst other wildfowl, the unusual sight of coastal birds such as Oystercatchers and Ringed Plover, which don't normally venture this far inland.

The track takes you through an enchanging wooded area past Halton, under the M6 and the Lune Aquaduct (B) carrying the Lancaster Canal over the River Lune. The latter was extremely difficult to construct due to the size of the bridge (600 ft long and 60ft high) and the continual flooding of the coffer dams during the building of the piers. John Rennie, the engineer, had worked with these difficulties before when constructing the London Bridge and Waterloo Bridge over the River Thames.

At the Forge Bank weir, 62 million gallons of water a day is taken from the river to feed the North West Water Authority system. Between the Lune Aquaduct and Skerton Bridge there is a second weir (C) which was completely reconstructed in 1976 to minimise the risk of tidal salt water flowing upstream.

They also keep a check on the numbers of Salmon and Sea Trout passing through by means of an electronic eye counter built into the weir.

The trail ends at Green Ayre Riverside Park (D) in Lancaster adjacent to Skerton Bridge, formerly the site of the Green Ayre Railway Station. A crane from a disused warehouse in Hornby has been erected in the park in memory of the 'little' North Western's Railway.

*Should you wish to continue your journey, either go across the Greyhound Bridge and take the cycle path to Morecambe or follow the cycle track beside the Greyhound Bridge on to St. George's Quay and to Glasson. (see 'Glasson Circular')*

*View of Ingleborough looking east from the bridge over the river Lune at Halton Green.*

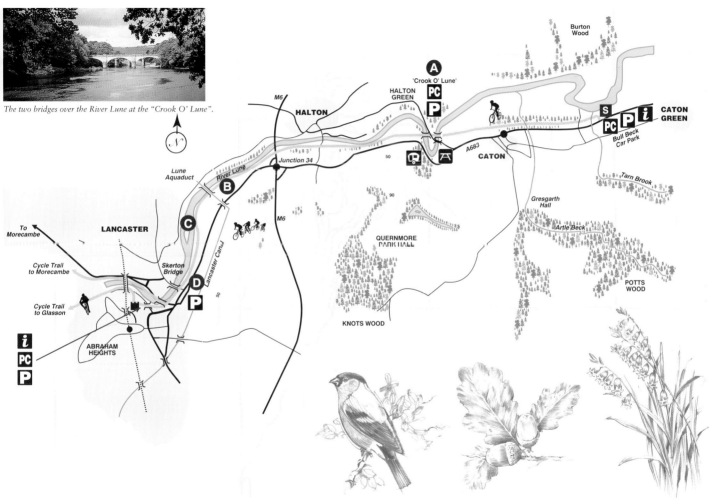

*The two bridges over the River Lune at the "Crook O' Lune".*

N

To Morecambe

Cycle Trail to Morecambe

Cycle Trail to Glasson

**LANCASTER**

Skerton Bridge

Lune Aqueduct

River Lune

Junction 34

M6

M6

**HALTON**

Lancaster Canal

ABRAHAM HEIGHTS

50

90

50

KNOTS WOOD

QUERNMORE PARK HALL

HALTON GREEN

'Crook O' Lune'

A683

CATON

Gresgarth Hall

Artle Beck

POTTS WOOD

Burton Wood

Tarn Brook

Bull Beck Car Park

**CATON GREEN**

*Bullfinch, Oak leaves with acorns and Bluebells.*

# LEVER PARK

LEVER PARK IS ALONGSIDE THE WEST BANK OF THE RIVINGTON RESERVOIRS ON THE SOUTH-WESTERN EDGE OF THE WEST PENNINE MOORS. THE M61 IS TO THE WEST OF THE RESERVOIRS AND THE TOWN OF HORWICH TO THE SOUTH.

**Lever Park is a very attractive area with an abundance of wild life around the Reservoirs even though it is situated so close to the towns of Horwich and Bolton. From Rivington Pike above the terraced gardens of Lever Park there are superb views of both Anglezarke and Rivington Moors, and Winter Hill.**

| START & FINISH: | S | The Barn (Information Centre) |
|---|---|---|
| MAP: | | O.S. Landranger Series No. 109 (Manchester) |
| LENGTH (approx): | | Route 1 12km (7 ½ m) Circular<br>Route 2 7km (4 ½ m) Circular |
| SURFACE: | | Tarmac, gravel, grass |
| RIDE RATING : | | Route 1  Park & Reservoirs  -  Easy<br>Route 2  Lever Park to the Pike - Moderate, adventurous<br>(From the Park to the Pike it is a steady climb) |

NOTE: *Cyclists must only use the routes with the blue posts, all other routes are for walkers only.*

Lever Park and the beautifully terraced gardens (A) as they are now, were created by William Hesketh Lever, but it was the Pilkington family who owned the estate for many generations previously. The terraced gardens rise from 80metres at reservoir level to 200metres at the Hall and have been planted with an amasing variety of shrubs and trees.

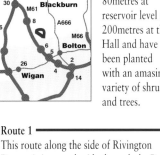

There are many varieties of birds to be seen through the Park also ducks and wading birds on the reservoir.

*Great Spotted Woodpecker.*

## Route 1 ▬▬▬

This route along the side of Rivington Reservoir is a gentle ride through the Park and around the upper half of the reservoir.

*Rivington Reservoir.*

## Route 2.

The route taking you through Lever Park and up to Rivington Pike (B) is a more testing one. This route is steep in places but the views from the Pike are tremendous and worth every minute of the climb.

Rivington Pike stands about 1,200 feet above sea level (approx 363m) This is the oldest tower in the South Pennines. It was constructed in 1733 by a John Andrews and is 17ft square and 20ft high. Before it was walled up it would have had a wooden roof, windows, a fireplace and a cellar. The Liverpool Corporation purchased the Pike in 1902 from Lord Leverhulme. When the corporation wanted to demolish it there was such a public outcry they left it standing.

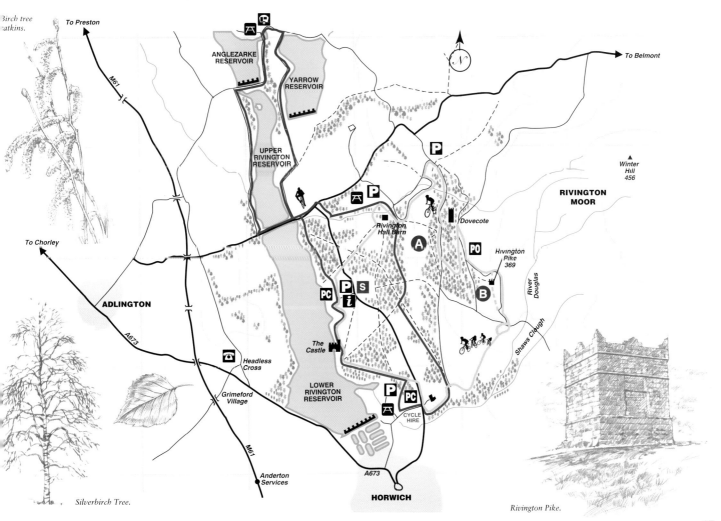

To Preston

Birch tree
catkins.

M61

ANGLEZARKE
RESERVOIR

YARROW
RESERVOIR

To Belmont

N

UPPER
RIVINGTON
RESERVOIR

Winter
Hill
456

RIVINGTON
MOOR

To Chorley

Rivington
Hall Barn

Dovecote

A

Hivington
Pike
369

PO

ADLINGTON

A673

River Douglas

B

PC

P  S
i

The
Castle

Headless
Cross

Shaws Clough

Grimeford
Village

LOWER
RIVINGTON
RESERVOIR

P

PC

CYCLE
HIRE

M61

Anderton
Services

A673

HORWICH

Silverbirch Tree.

Rivington Pike.

17

# DOWNHOLLAND TRAIL

THE DOWNHOLLAND TRAIL IS SITUATED BETWEEN AINSDALE, WHICH LIES BETWEEN SOUTHPORT AND FORMBY ON THE WEST COAST, TO LYDIATE, NORTH OF AINTREE IN MERSEYSIDE. THIS PATH IS THE BEGINNING OF THE TRAFFIC-FREE 'TRANS PENNINE TRAIL' WHICH WILL EVENTUALLY GO THROUGH TO HULL ON THE EAST COAST.

The Downholland Trail is very straight, travelling through the flat plains of East Lancashire. The path is mainly along the route of the old Cheshire Line Railway Co. which operated between Liverpool and Southport via Aintree. The railway's primary use was to take holiday makers to the coast from the Lancashire Mill towns.

| START: | S | Plex Moss Lane, Ainsdale off Formby by-pass (Signposted as a cycle path) |
|---|---|---|
| FINISH: | | Green Lane, Lydiate |
| MAP: | | O.S. Landranger Series No. 108 (Liverpool) |
| LENGTH (approx): | | 16km (10m) Linear |
| SURFACE: | | Ash, tarmac, forest path |
| RIDE RATING : | | Easy |

NOTE: *The trail can be continued to Liverpool*  — — — — —

KILOMETRES     1    2    3    4    5    6
STATUTE MILES      1       2       3       4

Although the start of this trail is at Plex Moss Lane, should you cross over the Formby bypass and carry straight on up the road for approximately 2kms you will come to the Irish Sea and Ainsdale Sands (**A**).

The Downholland Trail commences at Plex Moss Lane. Continue down this straight lane until you turn right at the Bridleway signpost indicating the track into the wood (**B**). The trail continues along a path until you turn left on to the route of the old Cheshire railway line (**C**). The section through the woods can be very muddy if the weather has been inclement.

The area around this trail is mainly cultivated farmland with the fields making an enchanting patchwork of colour throughout the changing seasons of the year.

After Fine Jane Pumping Station a stream runs parallel to the trail until it eventually joins the River Alt at Lydiate. Also in this section there is a separate bridleway path beside the trail.

*ACKNOWLEDGMENT : the exit from the railway to Plex Moss Lane is by kind permission of the John Moores Estate and the Church Commissioners.*

**LANCASHIRE**

Southport
Ainsdale
A570
A59
M6
Ormskirk 27
30
3
A565
7
M58
M57
2
M62
Liverpool
4    6    7

Hawthorne is commonly used for hedging.

Harvest mouse and Ox-eye Daisies.

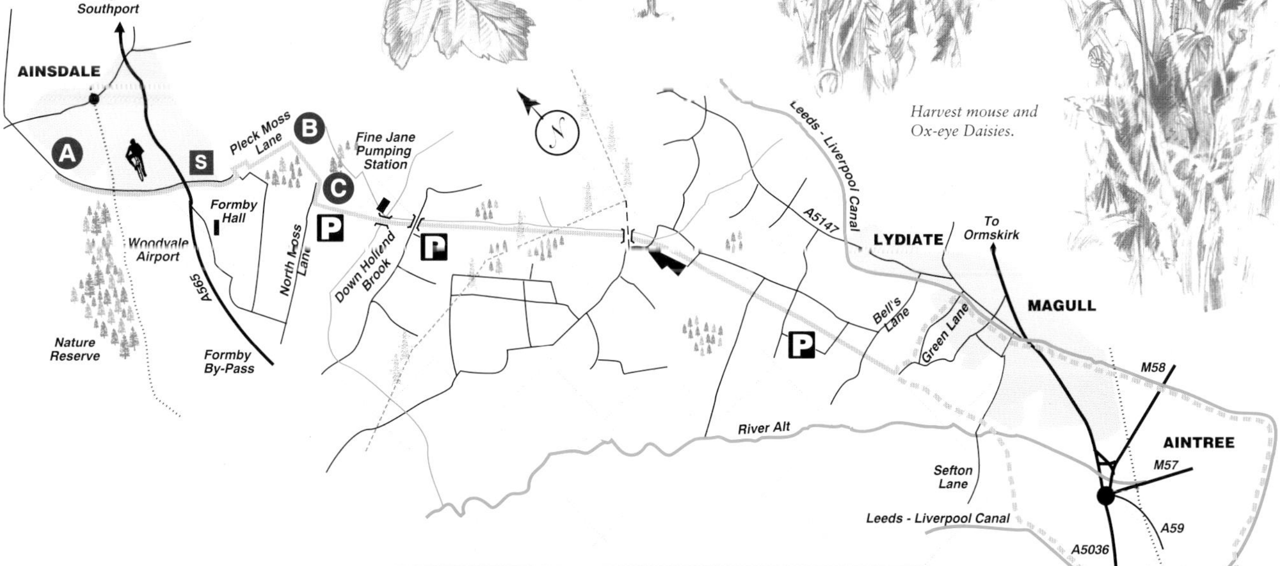

To Southport

AINSDALE

**A**

**S**

Pleck Moss Lane

**B**

Fine Jane Pumping Station

**C**

**P**

Formby Hall

North Moss Lane

**P**

Down Holland Brook

A565

Woodvale Airport

Nature Reserve

Formby By-Pass

Leeds - Liverpool Canal

A5147

LYDIATE

To Ormskirk

MAGULL

Bell's Lane

Green Lane

**P**

River Alt

Sefton Lane

Leeds - Liverpool Canal

M58

AINTREE

M57

A59

A5036

To Liverpool Loopline Cycle Track

To Litherland

The trail along the old Cheshire Lines railway track.

# WIGAN-BURSCOUGH

## CANAL TOW PATH

THIS TRAIL IS AN EXPERIMENTAL ROUTE FOR CYCLISTS ALONG PART OF THE LEEDS AND LIVERPOOL CANAL THROUGH THE VALLEY OF THE RIVER DOUGLAS BETWEEN WIGAN IN GREATER MANCHESTER AND BURSCOUGH IN WEST LANCASHIRE. NORTH OF THE M58 AND BETWEEN JUNCTIONS 26-27 ON THE M6

| | | |
|---|---|---|
| **START:** | **S** | Wigan Pier, Wigan |
| **FINISH:** | | New Lane, nr. Burscough |
| **MAPS:** | | O.S. Landranger Series No. 108 (Liverpool) |
| **LENGTH (approx):** | | 18km (11m) Linear |
| **SURFACE:** | | Gravel, grass, tarmac |
| **RIDE RATING :** | | Easy |

KILOMETRES 1 2 3 4 5 6
STATUTE MILES 1 2 3 4

The Leeds-Liverpool Canal which was completed in 1816 has 92 locks and is 141 miles long including its branches and took 46 years to construct. It is the longest single canal in the country and when linked with the Aire and Calder Navigation at Leeds forms a through route from the Irish Sea to the North Sea. In 1972 the last coal barges left the Plank Lane Colliery to Wigan power station.

The Trail starts in Wigan, whose charter dates back to 1246 and is one of Lancashire's oldest boroughs. Coal was the largest industry which in turn powered the mills in the surrounding areas of Lancashire. The Leeds-Liverpool canal transported cotton and coal from Wigan to Liverpool dock, also to the Midlands by way of the Leigh branch of the canal.

On leaving Wigan the trail route is between the Canal and the River Douglas

and, as you go under the M6 at Dean Locks (**A**), you can see four ages of transport. The M6 above you, the railway line and the canal on your right and the River Douglas on your left which used to carry coal to Preston before the canal was built.

Appley Bridge Locks (**B**) are the first locks the barges will encounter having left Liverpool on their way to Wigan. On the hilltop to the north is the village of Wrightington where the oldest Presbyterian church in England is sited.

At Parbold there was to have been a major canal junction but it was decided to route the canal through Wigan and Blackburn and all that remains is the drydock built on the site of the proposed junction. It is hard to believe that two hundred years ago there were coal mines, quarries and potteries in this area,

especially as this part of the Douglas valley is so picturesque. Residents along the canal bank have added to this attractive scene having planted flowers and shrubs along the towpath. At Newburgh the River Douglas turns northwards (**C**) and the canal carries on its way to Liverpool.

The Rufford branch (**D**) of the Leeds-Liverpool Canal joins the main arm of the canal before Burscough Bridge.

Three miles north of Burscough, an easy cycle ride along a minor road, is the Wildfowl Centre at Martin Mere (**E**). The Mere was created by a section of marsh remaining after the area was drained in 1787 and, as a result, geese and other wildfowl used this area for feeding and as a resting place during migration. The Wildfowl Trust bought the site in 1972 and is now a birdwatchers paradise.

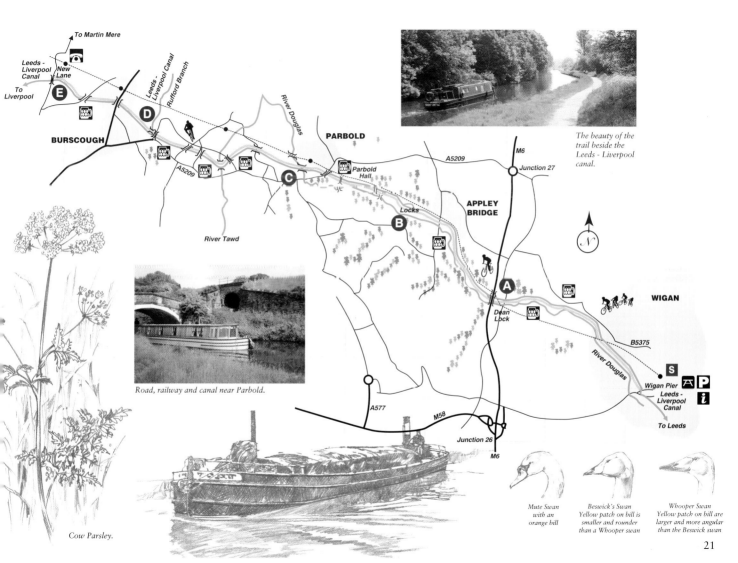

To Martin Mere

Leeds - Liverpool Canal

New Lane

To Liverpool

**E**

Leeds - Liverpool Canal

**D**

Leeds - Liverpool Canal

Rufford Branch

**BURSCOUGH**

A5209

River Douglas

River Tawd

**PARBOLD**

Parbold Hall

**C**

Locks

**B**

A5209

**APPLEY BRIDGE**

M6

Junction 27

N

**A**

Dean Lock

**WIGAN**

B5375

River Douglas

**S**

Wigan Pier
Leeds - Liverpool Canal

To Leeds

A577

M58

Junction 26

M6

The beauty of the trail beside the Leeds - Liverpool canal.

Road, railway and canal near Parbold.

Cow Parsley.

Mute Swan with an orange bill

Beswick's Swan Yellow patch on bill is smaller and rounder than a Whooper swan

Whooper Swan Yellow patch on bill are larger and more angular than the Beswick swan

# GRIZEDALE FOREST

*(meaning 'Valley of the Pigs')*

THIS MEANING COMES FROM THE VIKING INVADERS WHO FOUND MANY WILD BOAR IN THE FOREST, HENCE GRIZEDALE'S SYMBOL BEING THE BOAR GRIZEDALE FOREST IS CONTAINED TO THE NORTH AND EAST BY THE TOWN OF HAWKSHEAD AND ESTHWAITE WATER AND TO THE WEST BY CONISTON WATER.

**Grizedale, as in all lakeland forests, is a forest where there is a continuous process of felling and replanting trees. There are magnificent views of the distant fells to be seen from the high points, and delightful woodland glades that enhance the 30 miles of cycling tracks that take you through the 4,200 acres of this beautiful forest.**

| START & FINISH : | **S** | The Visitor's Centre, Grizedale Forest |
|---|---|---|
| **MAP:** | | O.S. Outdoor Leisure Series No. 6, English Lakes (S.E.) O.S. Outdoor Leisure Series No. 7, English Lakes (S.W.) |
| **LENGTH (approx):** | | **Red Route** (incorporating the Forest Park's Yellow and White waymarked routes) -12 km (7 ¹/₂ m) **Brown Route** (incorporating the Forest Park's Blue waymarked route) - 10 km (6 ¹/₂ m) |
| **SURFACE:** | | Forest paths and gravel |
| **RIDE RATING :** | | Easy, adventurous |

*NOTE: Be cautious as you travel along the tracks as this is a working forest, observe the warning signs and stay well clear of any working machinery.*

KILOMETRES    1    2    3
STATUTE MILES    1    2

The Estate, and Grizedale Hall which was built in the early part of the 20th Century, was owned by the Brocklebank family who controlled the Cunard Shipping Line. Many areas in the forest are named after places the Cunard ships visited. The Hall was used as a prisoner-of-war camp for German Officers in the Second World War, but was demolished in 1956.

The area was acquired by the Forestry Commission in 1936 and is now known as

The Grizedale Forest. This was the first of the Commission's forests to encourage recreational access by the public.

There are many cycle routes of which we have chosen two. All of which are within the boundary of the forest and where you will be able to see many of the magnificent sculptures, of which there are over 50 all made using the forest's natural stone and timber. Approximately 450 million years ago this area was covered by a shallow sea. This early period was known as the 'Silurian Epoch' and many of the forests, rocks, grey slates and shale were formed at this time. Also in the Gallery, which is a converted sawmill, you can watch some of the artists at work. It was in 1977 that the Grizedale Society began this scheme to provide a working environment for sculptors to use the forest

and all its elements to create natural works of art. In the 1960's the Society founded the 'Theatre in the Forest' which is renowned for its regular national and international musical events.

*The wildlife in the forest includes Red and Roe deer, Badgers, Foxes and the Red Squirrel. Sparrowhawks, Buzzards and Kestrels are frequently seen flying over the forest. The summer season brings an abundance of toadstools and wild strawberries and many species of dragonflies near the water.*

*Although now mainly conifer, the oldest trees of the forest are the Oak trees. Amongst the new plants to be seen are the bright pink willow herb and Silver Birch trees.*

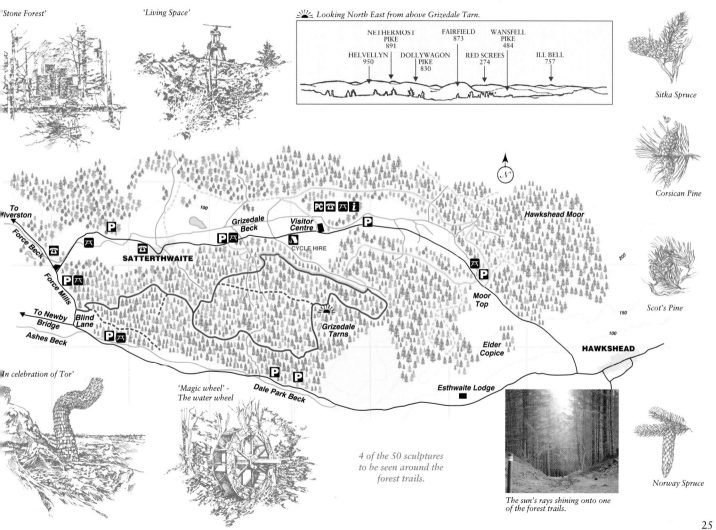

'Stone Forest'

'Living Space'

☼ Looking North East from above Grizedale Tarn.

NETHERMOST PIKE 891
FAIRFIELD 873
WANSFELL PIKE 484
HELVELLYN 950
DOLLYWAGON PIKE 830
RED SCREES 274
ILL BELL 757

Sitka Spruce

Corsican Pine

Scot's Pine

To Iverston

Force Beck

Force Mills

SATTERTHWAITE

Grizedale Beck

Visitor Centre

CYCLE HIRE

PC

Hawkshead Moor

Moor Top

100

200

150

100

To Newby Bridge

Blind Lane

Ashes Beck

Grizedale Tarns

Elder Copice

HAWKSHEAD

Dale Park Beck

Esthwaite Lodge

'In celebration of Tor'

'Magic wheel' - The water wheel

4 of the 50 sculptures to be seen around the forest trails.

The sun's rays shining onto one of the forest trails.

Norway Spruce

25

# ASKHAM FELL
## HEUGHSCAR HILL AND HELTONDALE BECK

ASKHAM FELL IS SITUATED BETWEEN ULLSWATER LAKE TO THE WEST THE RIVER LOWTHER TO THE EAST AND MOOR DIVOCK AND HELTONDALE TO THE SOUTH.

This wide and beautiful moorland looking out over Ullswater to Blencathra hill is crisscrossed with bridleways and accessible tracks. On these limestone fells there are a great many ancient cairns, burial mounds and stone circles. Through the fell runs 'High Street', the road the Romans built connecting their fort at Ambleside to Broughton outside Penrith.

| START & FINISH: | SA SB | Route 1  Roehead, S.E. of Pooley Bridge<br>Route 2  Dewpot Holes, Nr. Heltonhead |
|---|---|---|
| MAP: | | O.S. Outdoor Leisure Series No. 5<br>(The English Lakes, N.E.) |
| LENGTH (approx): | | Route 1. Heughscar Hill -  9 km (5 ½ m) Circular<br>Route 2. Heltondale Beck -  8 km (5 m) Circular |
| SURFACE: | | Grass, gravel, tarmac. |
| RIDE RATING : | | Route 1.  Moderate, adventurous<br>Route 2.  Easy, adventurous |

*NOTE: Be aware of the weather on these moorlands as the mist comes down very quickly on these open fells.*

KILOMETRES
STATUTE MILES

### Route 1 - Heughscar Hill
Commencing at Roehead the track goes through the gate and up the hill past the signpost for the Roman Road as it crosses your path to the second signpost at Moor Divock (A). Turn left to Askham making sure you keep slightly right going round the hill, not straight up Heughscar Hill! *(note: the trail is ill defined at this point)* When you are level with the trees which are further up the hill on your left, bearing right downhill towards a wood and a gate in the wall at Riggingleys Top (B). Follow the track beside the wall and before going over the cattle grid, turn left (C) up the path that eventually meets the minor road (D) where you turn left and left again at the first bridleway sign. Follow the path up the hill keeping Winder Hall Farm (E) on your right. As you gain height (F) you will be able to see behind you the remains of Lowther Castle.

The Lowther Estate has been in the Lonsdale family for seven generations. The fifth Earl, a great sportsman, gave the 'Lonsdale Belt' for boxing competitions. He was also known as the 'Yellow Earl' due to his yellow livery and owning a yellow Rolls Royce. In 1911 he became the first President of the Automobile Association (hence the AA's yellow livery)

### Route 2 - Heltondale Beck
This circular route around Heltondale Beck commences out of Heltonhead by the Dewpot holes where the bridleway crosses the track. This metal track takes you to the gates of a farm (1). Follow the bridleway to the ford over Heltondale Beck (2). Go through the ford and up through the gate in the wall. After the gate in the second wall keep left until you pick up the farm track. At Cockle Hill (3) turn left to the lovely village of Heltondale across the cattle grid and continue down to the road to Helton. Where the track meets the road (4) immediately take the left hand track signposted to 'Widewath Farm'. On the left are the farm buildings. Keep straight ahead between the stone walls. Go through the gate and follow the bracken path back to the Dewpot holes and the crossroads to Helton or Pooley Bridge.

*View south west towards Helvellyn from the trail from Roehead.*

LAKE DISTRICT

*Looking West from the track near Roehead.*

| PLACE FELL 657 | HALLIN FELL 388 | BIRKS 622 | HELVELLYN 950 | SHEFFIELD PIKE 675 | RAISE 883 | THE DODDS |
|---|---|---|---|---|---|---|

Lowther Castle

Lowther Park

**ASKHAM**

*Herdwick sheep.*

*Elder flower and berries.*

High Street (Roman Road)

**D**

**C**

200

**HELTON**

**E**

Winder Hill Farm

250

300

River Lowther

Barton House

Riggingleys Top

Heltonhead

**F**

**B**

**4**

200

Heughcar Hill 370

Dewpot Holes

Heltondale

To Bampton

*Meadow Cranesbill.*

300

350

**A**

**SB**

Wall

River Eamont

Howe Hill

High Street (Roman Road)

Roehead

Mossy Beck

200

300

Cockle Hill

**3**

**SA**

The Cockpit

Tarn Moor

Heltondale Beck

**P**

Pooley Bridge

B5320

**P** **i**

**P**

DUNMALLARD HILL

*Looking North West over Ullswater.*

BLENCATHRA 868

Scales Farm

**1**

400

**2**

**ULLSWATER**

Brown Beck

27

# THORNTHWAITE FOREST

THE THORNTHWAITE FOREST ASTRIDES THE WHINLATTER PASS WEST OF THE A66 AND BASSENTHWAITE LAKE AND EAST OF LORTON VALE IN THE NORTH WESTERN AREA OF THE LAKE DISTRICT.

The Thornthwaite Forest lies on either side of the Whinlattter Pass which formed part of the old 1761 Turnpike road between Keswick and Cockermouth. The Forest is the oldest Forestry Commission forest and was established in 1919 and created due to the shortage of wood after World War I. At the Visitors Centre there are films about the forest and a badger's sett to explore.

| START & FINISH: | **S** | Visitor's Centre off the Whinlatter Pass |
|---|---|---|
| MAP: | | O.S. Outdoor Leisure Series No. 4 (The English Lakes N.W.) |
| LENGTH (approx): | | Route 1. 11 ½ km (7 m) Circular<br>Route 2. 11 ½ km (7 m) Circular |
| SURFACE: | | Gravel, grass |
| RIDE RATING : | | Routes 1 & 2: Hard hills. Moderate tarmac roads. |
| CLIMBS: | | A long hard hill from the Visitors Centre to Junctions 1/3 Steep climbs in Darling How Plantation. |

NOTE: The tracks through the forest are not rights of way, therefore only the waymarked paths and the tracks of similar substance can be used.

KILOMETRES |

STATUTE MILES |

**LAKE DISTRICT**

The Forest's first plantings were south of the Whinlatter Pass towards Grisedale Pike (A) and were later extended north to the western banks of Bassenthwaite Lake (B), covering the fells of Graystones (C), Whinlatter (D) and Tarbarrel Moss (E) to the high point of Lord's Seat (552m) (F)

Pike (790m) to the south and Skiddaw (931m) to the west is reward enough for all the effort. The track takes you around the slopes of Lorton Fell and Whinlatter Hill (517m). At J27 it is worth a visit to the beautiful Spout Force Waterfall. If you are feeling very adventurous there are several steep climbs within the Darling How Plantation on the forest tracks.

For your return either rejoin the route at (J27) over Aiken Beck or join the Whinlatter Pass and turn right off the pass at (J32)where the trail runs parallel with the road to (J34) Comb Bridge. On joining the road turn left and return to the Visitors Centre.

worth a walk up the hill as the panoramic views are breathtaking from the dizzy heights of Skiddaw(931m) down to the town of Keswick and Derwent Water and around the hills taking in Borrowdale and Helvellyn.

*Grizedale Pike*

**HOW TO MEASURE THE HEIGHT OF A TREE.**

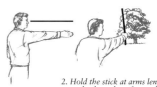

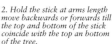

*1. Find a stick the same length as your arm.*

*2. Hold the stick at arms length move backwards or forwards till the top and bottom of the stick coincide with the top an bottom of the tree.*

*3. The distance from where you are standing to the tree is the height of the tree.*

## Route 1

From the Visitors Centre the trail commences from (J15) up a long hill to (J1), turn left continuing uphill to (J3). The views along this route are magnificent and on a clear day the sight of Grizedale

## Route 2

Starting at the Visitors Centre and turning left at (J15) make your way up the hill to (J1) and turn right. Before reaching (J9), on your right is Seat How. It is well

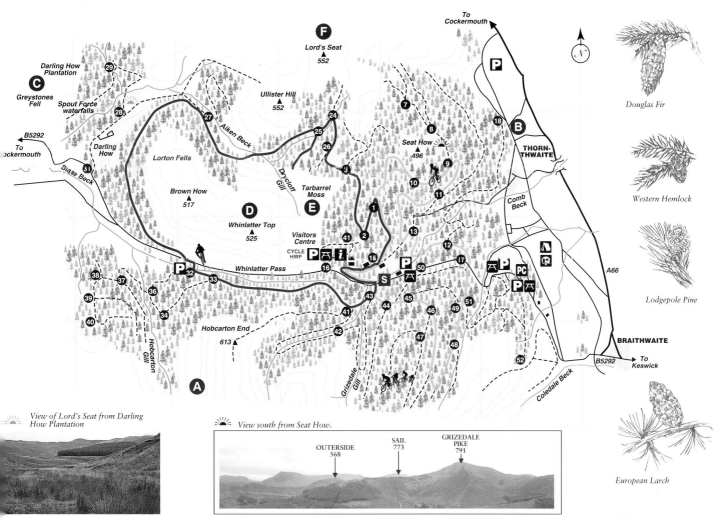

C **Greystones Fell**

**Darling How Plantation**

**Spout Force waterfalls**

B5292
To Cockermouth

Dyate Beck

**Darling How**

**Lorton Fells**

Aiken Beck

**Brown How**
517

D

**Whinlatter Top**
525

Dryclof Gill

E **Tarbarrel Moss**

**Visitors Centre**

CYCLE HIRE

**Whinlatter Pass**

Hobcarton Gill

**Hobcarton End**
613

A

F **Lord's Seat**
552

**Ullister Hill**
552

**Seat How**
496

Comb Beck

THORN-THWAITE

B

To Cockermouth

A66

Coledale Beck

**BRAITHWAITE**

B5292
To Keswick

Grizedale Gill

N

*Douglas Fir*

*Western Hemlock*

*Lodgepole Pine*

*European Larch*

*View of Lord's Seat from Darling How Plantation*

*View south from Seat How.*

OUTERSIDE
568

SAIL
773

GRIZEDALE PIKE
791

29

# WHITEHAVEN MINERAL TRAIL

THE WHITEHAVEN MINERAL TRAIL IS SITUATED BETWEEN WHITEHAVEN ON THE WEST
COAST OF CUMBRIA AND THE VILLAGE OF ROWRAH ON THE A5086.
THIS TRAIL IS THE BEGINNING OF THE 140 MILE "C2C" ROUTE TAKING YOU FROM
WHITEHAVEN TO SUNDERLAND

This trail passes several old mine buildings and quarries following the route of
the old Whitehaven to Rowrah mineral railway line which was built in the
1850's. The villages along this route grew very rapidly due to the coal, iron
ore and limestone industries in this region. Whitehaven became the third
busiest port in Britain during the early part of the 19th Century mainly due to
the shipping of these commodities.

| | | |
|---|---|---|
| START: | **S** | Calder Club, Esk Avenue, Whitehaven |
| FINISH: | | Sheriff's Gate near Lamplugh School, Kirkland |
| MAP: | | O.S. Landranger Series No. 86 (West Cumbria) |
| LENGTH (approx): | | 16km (10 m) |
| SURFACE : | | Ash, gravel |
| RIDE RATING: | | Easy |

KILOMETRES    1   2   3   4
STATUTE MILES    1   2   3

It is approx. 8k (5 miles) going down hill along the road from Kirkland to
the car park at Bowness Knott on the Lake side.

This trail is known as a 'Sculpture Trail' due to the 60 pieces of sculptured designs dotted along the route. There are sculptures, seats and marker posts commissioned from artists all over Britain. All these pieces of art have some connection with West Cumbria. Such as cast-iron beams from the old railway line that have been up-ended to serve as backs for the wooden seats. Sandstone seats with poems carved into the backs. Children from local schools were asked to do lots of drawings showing their favourite things in the area, such as insects, animals, birds, plants and quarries. These drawings then formed the basis for the shapes cut out in steel plate and mounted onto 8ft high marker posts.

By the end of the 1940's most of the quarries and mines had been abandoned and the railway line lay in disrepair until the Copeland Borough Council, West Cumbrian Groundwork Trust in partnership with Sustrans developed the trail.

The trail goes slightly uphill all the way to Kirkland through different areas of rock formation from sandstone at the coast to slates on the fells near Ennerdale.

Although this path comes to an end approximately 1/2 mile past Rowrah you can join an unclassified road. Instructions are given on a mile post as you leave the trail, taking you through Kirkland and on to Ennerdale Water via Croasdale.

**LAKE DISTRICT**

Workington
A66
Whitehaven
A5086
A595

*Meadow Pipit, Broom and a hedgehog.*

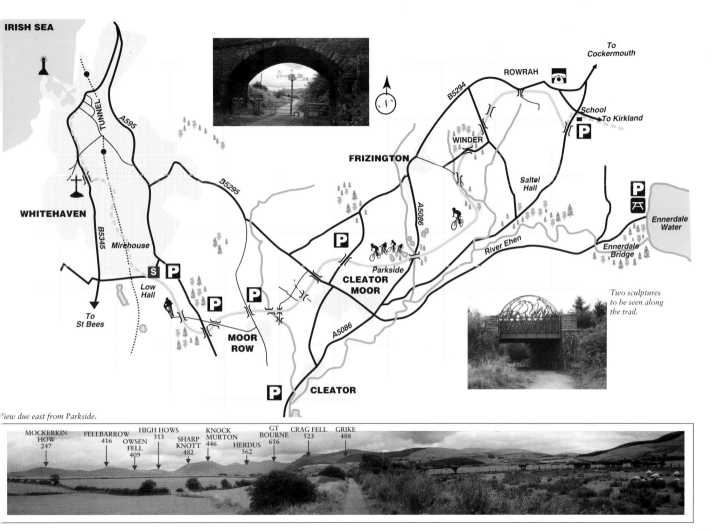

IRISH SEA

WHITEHAVEN

TUNNEL

A595

B5345

Mirehouse

Low Hall

To St Bees

MOOR ROW

S P

P

P

B5295

P

P

CLEATOR

P

CLEATOR MOOR

Parkside

A5086

A5086

FRIZINGTON

WINDER

ROWRAH

B5294

School

To Kirkland

To Cockermouth

Saltel Hall

River Ehen

Ennerdale Bridge

Ennerdale Water

P

P

Two sculptures to be seen along the trail.

*View due east from Parkside.*

MOCKERKIN HOW 247

FELLBARROW 416

OWSEN FELL 409

HIGH HOWS 313

SHARP KNOTT 482

KNOCK MURTON 446

HERDUS 562

GT BOURNE 616

CRAG FELL 523

GRIKE 488

# ENNERDALE FOREST

ENNERDALE FOREST IS SITUATED IN THE NORTH WESTERN HALF OF THE LAKE DISTRICT NATIONAL PARK BETWEEN LOWESWATER AND ENNERDALE FELL.

Ennerdale Water is the most westerly lake in the Lake District National Park, surrounded by some of the most spectacular mountain scenery to be seen in the Lake District. As there is no unauthorised vehicle access, the surrounding forest has a wonderful feeling of isolation.
The Forestry Commission acquired the land around the lake in 1926 and began planting the trees about a year later to form the basis of the forest we see today.

| START & FINISH: | **S** | Bowness Knott car park. |
|---|---|---|
| MAP: | | O.S. Landranger Series No. 89 (West Cumbria) or O.S. Outdoor Leisure Series No. 4 (The English Lakes N.W.) |
| LENGTH (approx): | | 20 km (12 ½ m) Circular |
| SURFACE : | | Tarmac, gravel. |
| RIDE RATING: | | Medium |

KILOMETRES          1          2          3          4
STATUTE MILES              1              2              3

At Ennerdale's head there are many volcanic crags. To the south is Great Gable (899m), with Kirk Fell (802m) and

**LAKE DISTRICT**

the huge towering mass of Pillar (892m) with Pillar rock in front of it, famous for its many rock climbs. To the west of Pillar are Steeple (819m) and Haycock (797m).

On the Northern side of the Water in front of Buttermere Fell there are many peaks of which Hay Stacks(597m), High Crag (744m), High Stile (806m) and Red Pike (755m) are the highest.

Along the northern side of EnnerdaleWater the trail leaves the car park with a gentle slope down to the lake side and, as you leave the lake behind the

River Liza flows beside the trail, the route climbs up going towards Black Sail Hut. Before reaching the Hut our path turns down the south side of the River Liza though the forest and goes back towards the Lake. Before reaching the Lake side there is a right hand turn taking you onto a Bridleway to go over the bridge across the River Liza and back up the northern side of the Lake to the Car Park at Bowness Knott.

*View of Pillar and the Valley of Ennerdale Water.*

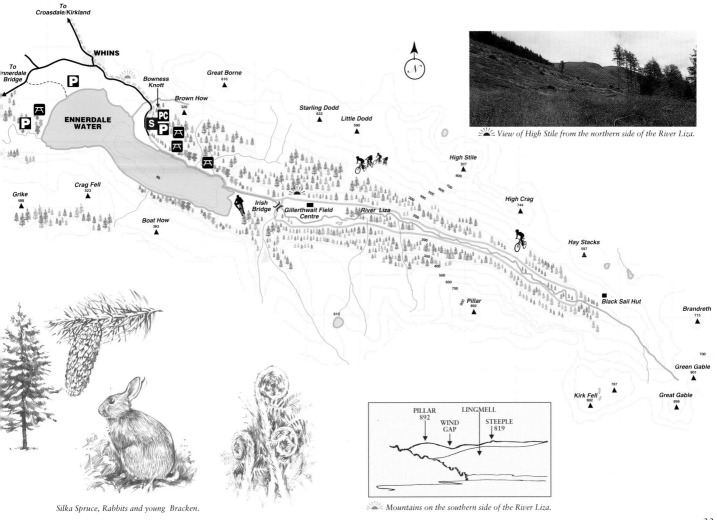

To Croasdale/Kirkland

WHINS

To Ennerdale Bridge

P

P

P

ENNERDALE WATER

S PC P

Bowness Knott

Brown How
320

Great Borne
616

Starling Dodd
633

Little Dodd
590

Great Borne

High Stile
807
800

View of High Stile from the northern side of the River Liza.

Grike
488

Crag Fell
523

Boat How
363

High Crag
744

Hay Stacks
597

Irish Bridge

Gillerthwaite Field Centre

River Liza

300
500
600
700

200

300

400

500

600

700

610

Pillar
892

800

Black Sail Hut

Brandreth
715

700

Green Gable
801

Kirk Fell
802

787

Great Gable
899

Silka Spruce, Rabbits and young Bracken.

PILLAR
892

LINGMELL

WIND GAP

STEEPLE
819

Mountains on the southern side of the River Liza.

33

# KENTMERE TRAILS

The Kentmere trails are situated between the Valley of Trout Beck to the west and Longsleddale Valley to the east. To the south runs the A591 from Kendal to Windermere.

**These trails take you over hills and moorlands of breathtaking beauty. Along the route to the village of Kentmere there are superb views of Black Sail and Crinkle Crags. Whereas going over Green Quarter Fell to the Longsleddale valley you will experience the wilderness of rough moorlands.**

| START & FINISH: | **S** | Staveley, Nr. Windermere |
| --- | --- | --- |
| MAP: | | O.S. Outdoor Leisure Series No. 7 (English Lakes, S.E.) |
| LENGTH (approx): | | Route 1. Kentmere Village   22km (14 m) Circular<br>Route 2. Green Quarter Fell   18km (11 m) Circular |
| SURFACE: | | Grass, tarmac, gravel |
| RIDE RATING : | | Route 1.  Moderate, adventurous<br>Route 2.  Hard |

NOTE: *The mist can roll over the fells of Green Quarter very quickly, be sure the weather forecast is good before starting this route.*

KILOMETRES    1    2    3    4
STATUTE MILES    1    2    3

## Route 1.

Starting at Staveley the road takes you to Barley Bridge (A) over the River Kent. Bare left keeping Barley Bridge and the river Kent on your right onto the lane to Ings. Turn right (B) on to a walled track where on a clear day there are magnificent views looking towards the hills of Black Sail, to Wrynose Pass and Crinkle Crags. Ford the stream of Park Beck and, as you round Whiteside End (C), there are superb views of the Kentmere Valley as it spreads out in front of you to the village of Kentmere at the head of the valley.

Kentmere Hall (D) is a superb farm building with a 14th century Pele tower. The tower would have been used as a look-out warning the inhabitants of the approach of Robert Bruce's Scottish raiders on their way south to Lancaster. In 1517 Bernard Gilpin was born here. He was a notorious leader of the Reformation and known as the 'Apostle of the North', later he became Archdeacon of Durham.

Although the lane heading north (E) out of Kentmere stops short of the Reservoir the valley is superb for stopping to have lunch maybe and admiring the hills around you.

## Route 2.

From Staveley the trail goes up the lane and right over Barley Bridge (1). Keep straight ahead and up onto Green Quarter Fell (2). The moorland is wild and beautiful as you pass Skeggles Water giving you a feeling of isolation before descending into the beautiful valley of Longsleddale. Turn right at Till's Hole (3), keeping the River Sprint on your left until you reach the three way branch of the track. Take the left hand path (4) up the hill and over the fell, fording Skeggleswater Dike (5) and returning either via the path beside the plantation (6) and the River Kent or go back down Hall Lane (7) to Staveley.

LAKE DISTRICT

Penrith
A66    10    A66
A592    M6
A591    Shap
A6    38
Ambleside
A593    Windermere    A591
Coniston    A591
A592    37
Newby    Kendal
Bridge

*Pony and traps along the trail to Kentmere.*

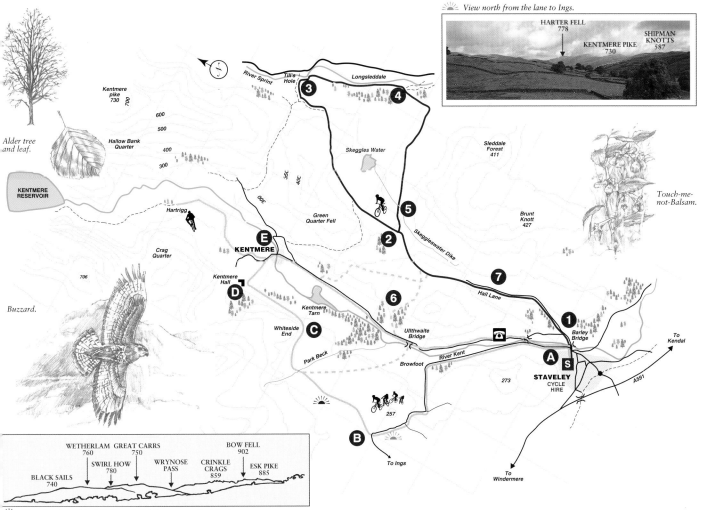

HARTER FELL
778

KENTMERE PIKE
730

SHIPMAN
KNOTTS
587

River Sprint

Till's Hole

Longsleddale

**3**

**4**

Kentmere
pike
730      700

600

500

400

300

Hallow Bank
Quarter

Skeggles Water

Sleddale
Forest
411

KENTMERE
RESERVOIR

Hartrigg

550

400

300

Green
Quarter Fell

Brunt
Knott
427

Touch-me-
not-Balsam.

Alder tree
and leaf.

**5**

Skeggleswater Dike

**E**
KENTMERE

Crag
Quarter

**2**

Kentmere
Hall

**D**

**7**

Hall Lane

706

Kentmere
Tarn

**6**

Buzzard.

Whiteside
End

**C**

Ullthwaite
Bridge

**1**

Barley
Bridge

To
Kendal

Park Beck

Browfoot

River Kent

273

**A**
**S**

STAVELEY
CYCLE
HIRE

A591

257

**B**

To Ings

To
Windermere

WETHERLAM  GREAT CARRS
760           750

BOW FELL
902

SWIRL HOW
780

WRYNOSE
PASS

CRINKLE
CRAGS
859

ESK PIKE
885

BLACK SAILS
740

Westerley view of the hills from the bridleways near Park Beck.

35

# CYCLE HIRE CENTRES

*The following is a list of cycle hire centres. Intending hirers should telephone for opening times and types of bikes available.*

## LANCASHIRE

**BOLTON MOUNTAIN BIKES**
247 BLACKBURN ROAD,
EGERTON,
BOLTON BL7 3SN
TEL: 0204 594418

**• MOUNTAIN BIKES**
LEVER PARK AVENUE,
HORWICH
TEL: 0204 847759

**PEDAL POWER**
**MOUNTAIN BIKE HIRE,**
WADDINGTON ROAD,
(NR. ROUNDABOURT)
CLITHEROE
TEL: 0200 22066

**D. TOURS, (TANDONS ONLY)**
49 HOPE STREET NORTH,
HORWICH,
BOLTON
TEL: 0204 699460

**MIKES BIKES,**
UNIT ONE,
ALICE ST.
MORCAMBE LA2 5NH
TEL: 0524 425132

## LAKES DISTRICT

**BIKES-2-U**
**(BIKES BROUGHT TO YOU FOR HIRE)**
KESWICK
TEL: 07687 78023
MOBILE PHONE  0836 331564
                         0831 669671

**• WHINLATTER FOREST PARK**
**MOUNTAIN BIKE HIRE**
THORNTHWAITE FOREST
TEL: 07687 78023

**• WHEELBASE**
STAVELEY
STAVELEY MILL YARD
TEL: 0539 821443

**• WHEELBASE**
GRIZEDALE FOREST PARK
TEL: 0229 860369

**MOUNTAIN BIKE HIRE**
KESWICK MOUNTAIN BIKES
SOUTHEY HALL,
KESWICK
CA12 5ND
TEL: 07687 75202

**GHYLLSIDE CYCLES**
THE SLACK,
AMBLESIDE
TEL: 05394 33592

**WINDERMERE LAKELAND LEISURE,**
**MOUNTAIN BIKE HIRE**
TEL: 05394 44786
WINDERMERE
(OPP. WINDERMERE RAILWAY STATION)

*• CYCLE HIRE CENTRE INDICATED ON*
*THE MAP.*

# HOW TO ENTER FOR YOUR WILDE'S CERTIFICATE

As you complete each route fill in the form overleaf in the appropriate place. When it is completed send it together with a postal order for £1.50 made out to Gildersleve Publishing to:-

**GILLIAN ROWAN-WILDE**
Gildersleve Publishing Ltd
Capricorn House
Blackburn Road
Rising Bridge
Lancashire   BB5 2AA

Name:..........................................................................

Address:......................................................................

.....................................................................................

.....................................................................................

............................................... Age: ...........................

Signed: .......................................................................

Model of bike and date purchased:

.....................................................................................

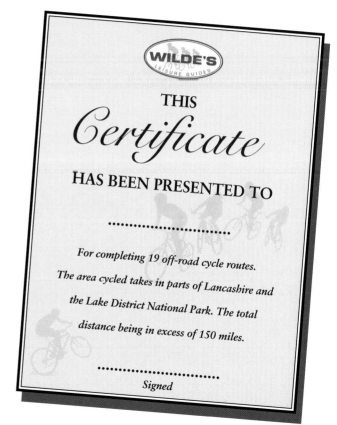

THIS

*Certificate*

## HAS BEEN PRESENTED TO

.............................

For completing 19 off-road cycle routes. The area cycled takes in parts of Lancashire and the Lake District National Park. The total distance being in excess of 150 miles.

.............................

*Signed*

| ROUTE | DATE RIDE COMPLETED | TIME TAKEN | COMMENTS ON THE ROUTE |
|---|---|---|---|
| 1. Dunsop Bridge | | | |
| 2. Gisburn Forest Route 1 | | | |
| 3. Gisburn Forest Route 2 | | | |
| 4. Glasson Circular | | | |
| 5. Bull Beck - Lancaster | | | |
| 6. Lever Park Route 1 | | | |
| 7. Lever Park Route 2 | | | |
| 8. Wigan - Burscough | | | |
| 9. Downholland Trail | | | |
| 10. Grizedale Forest Route 1 | | | |
| 11. Grizedale Forest Route 2 | | | |
| 12. Askham Fell Route 1 | | | |
| 13. Askham Fell Route 2 | | | |
| 14. Thornthwaite Forest Route 1 | | | |
| 15. Thornthwaite Forest Route 2 | | | |
| 16. Whitehaven Mineral Trail | | | |
| 17. Ennerdale Forest | | | |
| 18. Kentmere Trails Route 1 | | | |
| 19. Kentmere Trails Route 2 | | | |

WILDE'S
LEISURE GUIDES

# HELP CREATE A TRAFFIC-FREE NETWORK...
## Roads for people

- The figures speak for themselves. Over 20 million cars are registered in Britain and road traffic is projected to at least DOUBLE by the year 2025.

- Twice as much traffic on our roads.... What an appalling prospect!

- And the more cars there are, the more unpleasant it gets to travel by bike or on foot.

- But now, an alternative to the miseries of traffic-choked roads is being created...

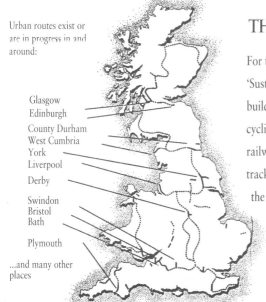

Urban routes exist or are in progress in and around:

Glasgow
Edinburgh
County Durham
West Cumbria
York
Liverpool
Derby
Swindon
Bristol
Bath
Plymouth

...and many other places

## THE SUSTRANS TRAFFIC-FREE NETWORK

For ten years, Sustrans - it stands for 'Sustainable Transport' - has been building new traffic-free routes for cyclists and walkers, using disused railway lines, canal towpaths, forest tracks and riversides - often through the heart of towns and cities - linked to minor roads and open spaces.

The Sustrans paths are designed to make travel safer, healthier and more friendly for people and wildlife. They cut right through congestion and pollution. They are built where the need is greatest - in towns and cities with links to the countryside.

*You can help bring about a complete national network! See overleaf for details.*

KEY: _____ Routes completed or in progress
........ Main Sustrans proposals

**sustrans**
PATHS FOR PEOPLE

# PLEASE JOIN SUSTRANS - AND HELP CREATE MORE TRAFFIC-FREE ROUTES

More public support and activity is needed to achieve a true national network. Without donations from the public, the routes simply would not happen.

Your contribution will be directly used to start new paths countrywide. Once we have done the initial work, we can often secure grants to cover the construction cost.

If you can give a donation, please be generous and in particular, consider making a regular commitment of a few pounds each month, to provide an income we can rely on.

Please use the Sustrans paths and tell others about them.

Sustrans routes are in progress between Dover and Inverness, between Bristol and London, across the Pennines and elsewhere.

PATRONS INCLUDE:
Chris Boardman • Dr Mayer Hillman • Dervia Murphy • Bill Oddie
Jeremy Paxman • Jonathan Porritt

## sustrans
### PATHS FOR PEOPLE

HEAD OFFICE 35 King Street, Bristol BS1 4DZ Tel: 0272 268893
SCOTLAND 53 Cochrane Street, Glasgow G1 1HL Tel: 041 552 8241
NORTH EAST Rockwood House, Barn Hill, Stanley, Co Durham DH9 8AN Tel: 0207 281259

Registered Charity No 326550  Company Limited by Guarantee No 1797726
VAT Registration No 416740656

## Yes I'll join
Set of lovely Sustrans postcards free when you join

NAME ..............................................................
ADDRESS .........................................................
.........................................................................
POSTCODE ................................ PHONE ...................
[ ] Please send information about Sustrans routes near me.

### EITHER
YES I'll join with a donation of:
[£15] [£25] [£50] [£100] [£ ____ other] (please tick)

Please EITHER enclose cheque/PO payable to SUSTRANS OR complete you Access/Visa No. here and sign:

Card Expiry Date ................................................
Signature .................................... Date ...................

———————— /———————— /———————— /————————

### AND/OR
Even better for Sustrans, join with a regular monthly payment. We will send a beautiful wallmap of the paths - plus postcards - to thank you for your standing order of £3 a month or more.

YES I'll join with a monthly standing order of:
[£3] [£5] [£10] [£15] [£25]
[£_____other] (please tick)

NAME OF MY BANK .............................................
ADDRESS OF MY BANK .........................................

Current Acc No _/_/_/_/_/_/_/_/_/_/
Bank Sort Code _/_/_-_/_/_-_/_/_/

MY NAME ........................................................
Signature .................................... Date ...................

DON'T FORGET TO COMPLETE YOUR OWN ADDRESS ABOVE!
REMEMBER You can cancel this standing order at any time by informing your bank.
BANK INSTRUCTIONS: Please pay the above sum on the 1st next and monthly thereafter to SUSTRANS, Acc No 1400978, Lloyds Bank, 55 Corn St, Bristol BS99 7LE.
Sort Code 30-00-01. Please quote ref:

POST TO SUSTRANS, FREEPOST BS7739, Bristol, BS1 4BR.
No stamp is required although it will save us paying postage if you use one.
*Thank you*